Series by Stephen Kagarise

Hysterion: Surrealist Love Poems

Zombie Chronicles

The Diary of Madame Rentz

Cyberpunk 1876

Approved Jawbone

KISS CONTAGION

KISS CONTAGION

Stephen Kagarise

Hysterion Press

ISBN : 979-8-9992019-7-3

"What must be shall be."

— Juliet

CONTENTS

Placed to the Best Advantage

See to it, says the Watchman, and if
people are found complaining so soon,
what's the use for such a sister state
of things? Be satisfied, whether it be
satisfactory or not. The company
which he represents is advancing apace
upon us, hence the delay in his veins,
or else he'd have a good time for once.
It must be made to correspond with
fiery dragons and solemn processions.

All the Elements of Permanency

Money and muscle bottom in one
body, so artful and insidious as
an entering wedge. Now is the time for
its confluence more exclusively in
this direction. The trade will continue
and enlarge, as something merely
auxiliary to the local systems in force.
I would like to know what becomes
of profundity. On its face it looks
innocent enough in its phraseology.

Where Labor Reigns Supreme

It is not my habit to indulge in
personalities, and thus cause mighty
organic or spiritual changes. Just
so it was in this case, for I could have
consumed the time in intimating
wild and bare, and returns promptly
made where wanted. But those advantages
sacrifice the truth to ecstatics, after
thus disposing of the difference in
attraction for his own selfish pleasure.

To Suit the Most Fastidious Taste

The fewer of such men we have,
the better. Since his visit to these parts,
there are several literally black with
grief, which they found to be a flat surface
below more lovely riffles. Hodgson
and a comrade had that abominable gag
a dozen times repeated, and the edge
is very abrupt, if we have nothing more
substantial to offer. Combined, they
form a bill of fare five times that number.

Coining Money with Their Work

A glass of whisky fires the brain
with all proper and possible celerity.
Tit for tat works wonders, dancing
through the day to note the compliments.
One or two handsome girls, within
the reach of all, began a desultory talk,
quite to the consternation of a gang
of drunken roughs. Where it came from
is a mystery. Under protest and with
wry faces, those Prima Donnas dance.

The Ideas of Approved Croakers

A young tyro is getting along nicely,
believing all the yarns told him by the man
who has just returned with a lady like
sunrise without a dawn. He made such a
splurge and stutter in the start, while
her singing put a calliope on the venture.
He views his coming very pleasantly,
and says that it will be cause for rejoicing
to make one vast monopoly. What he
meant to say is quoted quite extensively.

Does Your Jurisdiction Extend Over Us?

She points with pride to the products
of her great and useless commotion among
the people. None other genuine, every
arrangement made for special attention.
Before Mosby and since Mosby, it is
useless to prosecute the masters by hurling
a round shot of 450 pounds. She taps
one of the finest—others soon will follow.
A stinking puppy in human shape was
summarily disposed of his win-spr-summer.

Hastening to Escape the Shadows

What a mixing up was there, between
Buttercup and the Captain. His eyes flash
fire, and don't you forget how such a
nice dish of strawberries levels all ranks.
Courting a fray makes us friends with
him at once, satisfied that the occurrence
was unavoidable. He will get a glimpse
of a failing of his own, and nobody see him
serve in so many places at one time, as
the only man to please his obliging chorus.

Once I Was a Maiden Blithe and Free

The Infinite has sowed his name in
burning stars, each one doing all he can
to charm his Dulcinea. Drunks began
early last evening to pour into Madame
all that is required to work the pedals,
and thus the music rolls from the strings.
A full-blown rose "besprinkled" with
the purest dew will be given to each on
this stretch, before they twist and turn
about to cast love glances o'er the way.

Thousands of Ourselves Forgotten

Forty-two was the highest number
thrown at the lucky Dom, for they must be
sold to be remembered or forgotten.
More than half the ladies will be pleased to
receive calls today, to discharge certain
duties. Still, it is the humor of the thing
to humor them. Shall scrutiny impose into
the manner of their stewardship? If they
are in it, well. If they are out of it, well,
what then? We endure our allotted span.

A Tame Way of Expressing the Matter

Miss Calla may well feel proud of his company, for attentions and the pleasure afforded by the situation. Carnations acted as ushers, adapted to this climate to enhance its interests. Although he never "let his left hand know what his right hand did," he will commence at once a very pleasant and social gathering. Rounds of applause and roars of laughter greeted every one of the different acts.

Competitive Suggestions of Acts

She plunged wildly and madly into
the current of fashionable pleasure,
a motley collection of foul and loathsome
combinations that no person covers
all of. It varies in style from four legs
and a tail, up to the eloquent tribute
clothed with thunder and the glory of his
nostrils. It will now be handy to drop
in something we have made reference to.
Starch half lime under a similar name.

Rules for Telling the Ordinary Dose

Bonanza influences are steadily
at work, the passage strong and variable.
Such is but justice, and in compliance
with a long course of misrule. I always
feel happy when every man has a new
suit of clothes. With this simple addition
no more jawbone is wanted from us.
We propose to keep on at the same rate.
What pleasure it is to pay one's debts
that swiftly glide into the twilight gray.

Twenty Minutes Out of Reckoning

As to what natural phenomenon was
to take place at this time, or which dire
calamities are to disturb the elements,
these fearful prognostics may all prove true.
Very pronounced twinkling indicates
either commotion in the upper regions,
or a sudden fall of temperature there.
He comes as near to such nonsense as he
can, again making a noise with his pet
gasconade and terrible gripes of jealousy.

Polished Steel Surface and Springs

A new plan had been adopted, to be
put in force as soon as the idea of
going en masse made it practicable.
The face is not a mask but a mirror.
You cannot stamp the marks, the lines,
the flowing curves of the agreeable.
In place of attraction, there is repulsion.
A kind of veil covers the contact of
warm breath, but it is in fact nothing
else than a specialty made of steam.

With Little Force and Great Kindness

Ah, those terrible tongues of ours.
Are we half aware of their mighty powers?
Somebody's glass goes smash, stirred by
a sneer, a shrug, a whisper low. The lips
may curl with a careless smile, when a man's
skeleton is put by her side. That night he
will tell where the best bargains are to
be had, and just what merchants are alive
and doing business. Nor let it be said I
watch and wait by the close, locked gate.

Attempting to Hold the Supremacy

The times demand it, like Minerva
from the cleft head of Jove, and no terms
of peace until he prays God "the day
be not far distant." Twelve men, five in
one heap, and seven in another, were
all divested of clothing. The constitution
and wants of this numerous class are
not new and untried, but, having been
tested by wide and constant use, do rise up
and bless a thing for worms to feed on.

Completely Overturned and Set Aside

I cannot forego the pleasure which
it affords me, now the barriers are being
removed. They may make solid earth
when this shall have been done, and like
Simeon of old exclaim, "Lettest now
thy servant depart, for mine eyes have seen
the glory." He will accommodate you
at the tin shop "round the corner," to any
length and full measure, and we direct
that which nature has lavished upon us.

In the Minds of the New Purchasers

Thus the triangular fight begins to
close at that place, and at the same time
the most enjoyable entertainments.
A brilliant olio of gems is kept warm
and lighted evenings, and hot water
apparatus which gives the symptoms.
Laid bare under this act, we let their
houses fall into decay, and thus the poor
gentlemen meet me and pay, that we
may pay others rectified by the action.

Never Contented in a Cold Climate

Sad havoc leaves a partial vacuum,
conveying the heat to their limbs before
reaching the heated slopes. He knew
of no better locality to build up, hence
our interview often travels backwards
to the land of the setting sun. How much
we do miss its native haunts as matters
of importance. With this difference, that as
the sun withdraws its rays, the fool's
errand leaves a balsam of wild cherry.

A Surrounding Guard of Superlatives

Sometimes an enraged Big Brother
arrives after the ceremony is over,
and proceeds to vent his rage, or even
offer violence. The nightmare hath
his change of front, for then I know I have
a strong, though silent, orator. Lack
of water moved briskly, painted white
on the outside and red on the inside.
War is declared without further notice.
Ye must pay, whosoever neglecteth.

Probably few people would object to the doctrine of a—that is to say, a—how shall we put it? well, a warm hereafter, as it were; provided they had the selection of the people to go there.

The Daily Astorian, February 9, 1879

SPECIAL THANKS TO

D. C. Ireland, Publisher of *The Daily Astorian*

and the University of Oregon Libraries

COVER ART

Car of Love or Love's Wayfaring,

Study of Maria Zambaco

by Sir Edward Burne-Jones

www.ingramcontent.com/pod-product-compliance
Lightning Source LLC
LaVergne TN
LVHW010946110826
845149LV00013B/2772

* 9 7 9 8 9 9 9 2 0 1 9 7 3 *